Place Value through Hundred Thousands

hundred-thousands
ten-thousands
one-thousands
hundreds
tens
ones

761,605

The area of all the land in Mexico is **761,605** square miles.
expanded form: 700,000 + 60,000 + 1,000 + 600 + 5
standard form: 761,605
word name: seven hundred sixty-one thousand, six hundred five

---

Write each number in **standard form.**

1. 50,000 + 7,000 + 200 + 60 + 9   57,269

2. 300,000 + 5,000 + 800 + 6   305,806

3. 700,000 + 40,000 + 50 + 3   740,53

Write each number in **expanded form.**

4. 34,562   30,000 + 4,000 + 500 + 60 + 2

5. 621,700   600,000 + 2

6. 403,087 _____

Write the **word name** for each number.

7. 35,621 _____

8. 246,809 _____

Place Value through Hundred Millions

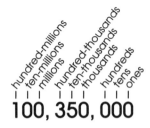

hundred-millions
ten-millions
millions
hundred-thousands
ten-thousands
thousands
hundreds
tens
ones

100, 350, 000

Mexico has more than **100,350,000** people.
word name: one hundred million, three hundred fifty thousand

Write each number in **standard form**.

1. nine million, one hundred three thousand, two hundred five

   _____

2. four hundred thirty-three million, six hundred forty-seven thousand, one hundred twelve

   _____

3. seventeen million, two hundred twenty-one thousand, fifty

   _____

Tell the **place value** of the **7** in each number.

4. 379, 882, 154 _____

5. 17, 205, 148 _____

6. 2, 057, 268 _____

7. 508, 672, 304 _____

8. 540, 916, 278 _____

9. 789, 544, 912 _____

Compare and Order Numbers

Compare **3,783** and **3,698**

Begin at the left. Find the first place where
the digits are different. Then compare.

< means **less than**
> means **greater than**
= means **equal to**

The sign points to the
number that is less.

3, 783
3, 698
↑
7 hundreds > 6 hundreds   3, 783 > 3, 698

Compare the numbers. Write <, >, or = in the ◯.

1.   687 ◯ 593

5,213 ◯ 8,436

7,549 ◯ 9,264

2.   254 ◯ 221

3,333 ◯ 3,491

9,054 ◯ 9,268

3.   8 8 ◯ 6 10

20 6 ◯ 2 7

10 9 ◯ 5 5

Write the numbers in **order** from **least** to **greatest**.

4. 149 822 324 287   _____

5. 2,973 3,006 2,118 3,652   _____

6. 4,431 2,840 4,931 2,821   _____

Problem Solving

7. Three girls were in a race. Juanita ran **135** yards, Maria ran **460** yards,
   and Lucia ran **310** yards. Mark the distances on the number line.
   Then write the names of the girls on the blanks.

←———+————————+————————+————————+————————+———→
      100   200   300   400   500

_____   _____   _____

Round to the Nearest Ten or Hundred

To round numbers to the nearest ten, look at the **ones** place.

Round **583** to the nearest ten.
583 is between **580** and **590**.

583

↑
round *down*

To round numbers to the nearest hundred, look at the **tens** place.

Round **583** to the nearest hundred.
583 is between **500** and **600**.

583

↑
round *up*

When the number you are looking at is 5 through 9, round up.

583 rounds to **580**.

583 rounds to **600**.

Round each number **to the nearest ten.**

1. 43 _____   85 _____   62 _____

2. 386 _____   251 _____   805 _____

3. 1,283 _____   4,065 _____   8,763 _____

Round each number **to the nearest hundred.**

4. 378 _____   542 _____   439 _____

5. 1,894 _____   2,538 _____   7,509 _____

6. 109 _____   85 _____   47 _____

Challenge

Round each amount of money to the nearest dollar.

7. $1.79 _____ $8.35 _____ $27.55 _____

Hint: Look at the number to the right of the number you are rounding to.

Round to the Nearest Thousand

To round numbers **to the nearest thousand**, look at the **hundreds** place.

Round **4,506** to the nearest thousand.
4,506 is between **4,000** and **5,000**.

4,506
↑
round *up*

4,506 rounds to 5,000.

Round **37,195** to the nearest thousand.
37,095 is between **37,000** and **38,000**.

37,195
↑
round *down*

37,195 rounds to 37,000.

Round each number **to the nearest thousand.**

1. 3,468 _____   6,843 _____   7,540 _____

2. 15,033 _____   40,909 _____   29,895 _____

3. 942 _____   458 _____   99 _____

4. Mexico has many volcanoes. Some have erupted in recent years while others lay dormant. Round the height of each volcano to the nearest thousand.

    Pico de Orizaba 18,555 _____   **Popocatépeti** 17,930 _____

    Colima 12,361 _____   **El Chichón** 7,300 _____

Challenge

5. The area of all the land in Mexico is **761,605** square miles.
    Round the number to the nearest place given below.

    ten _____   hundred _____

    thousand _____   ten thousand _____

    hundred thousand _____   million _____

Add with One Regrouping

Add the **ones**. Regroup as needed.	Add the **tens**. Regroup as needed.	Add the **hundreds**.	Estimate:
$\begin{array}{r} 34\boxed{6} \\ + 58\boxed{2} \\ \hline \boxed{8} \end{array}$	$\begin{array}{r} {}^{1} \\ 3\boxed{4}6 \\ + 5\boxed{8}2 \\ \hline \boxed{2}8 \end{array}$	$\begin{array}{r} {}^{1} \\ \boxed{3}46 \\ + \boxed{5}82 \\ \hline \boxed{9}28 \end{array}$	$\begin{array}{r} 300 \\ + 600 \\ \hline 900 \end{array}$
$6 + 2 = $ **8 ones**	$4 + 8 = $ **12 tens** **12 tens** is **1 hundred** and **2 tens**	$1 + 3 + 5 = $ **9 hundreds** The **sum** is **928**.	Remember: $\begin{array}{r} 346 \leftarrow \text{addend} \\ + 582 \leftarrow \text{addend} \\ \hline 928 \leftarrow \text{sum} \end{array}$

Add. Regroup as needed.

1.
$\begin{array}{r} 68 \\ + 13 \\ \hline \end{array}$
$\qquad$
$\begin{array}{r} 23 \\ + 58 \\ \hline \end{array}$
$\qquad$
$\begin{array}{r} 53 \\ + 19 \\ \hline \end{array}$
$\qquad$
$\begin{array}{r} 47 \\ + 26 \\ \hline \end{array}$

2.
$\begin{array}{r} 654 \\ + 138 \\ \hline \end{array}$
$\qquad$
$\begin{array}{r} 321 \\ + 581 \\ \hline \end{array}$
$\qquad$
$\begin{array}{r} 841 \\ + 109 \\ \hline \end{array}$
$\qquad$
$\begin{array}{r} 924 \\ + 39 \\ \hline \end{array}$

3.
$\begin{array}{r} 3,407 \\ + 1,225 \\ \hline \end{array}$
$\qquad$
$\begin{array}{r} 6,295 \\ + 2,063 \\ \hline \end{array}$
$\qquad$
$\begin{array}{r} 2,457 \\ + 3,831 \\ \hline \end{array}$
$\qquad$
$\begin{array}{r} 8,536 \\ + 1,092 \\ \hline \end{array}$

4. The boys' soccer team practiced for **45** minutes on Monday and **45** minutes on Wednesday. How many minutes did they practice in all?

5. There were **365** red apples and **283** green apples at the market. How many in all?

_____

_____

Add with More Regroupings

Add the **ones**.
Regroup as
needed.

$$
\begin{array}{r}
3,75\overset{1}{4} \\
+\ 1,837 \\
\hline
1
\end{array}
$$

Add the **tens**.
Regroup as
needed.

$$
\begin{array}{r}
3,7\overset{1}{5}4 \\
+\ 1,837 \\
\hline
91
\end{array}
$$

Add the **hundreds**.
Regroup as
needed.

$$
\begin{array}{r}
3,\overset{1}{7}54 \\
+\ 1,\overset{1}{8}37 \\
\hline
591
\end{array}
$$

Add the **thousands**.

$$
\begin{array}{r}
\overset{1}{3},754 \\
+\ \overset{1}{1},837 \\
\hline
5,591
\end{array}
$$

Add. Regroup as needed.

1.
$$
\begin{array}{r} 368 \\ +593 \\ \hline \end{array}
\qquad
\begin{array}{r} 593 \\ +668 \\ \hline \end{array}
\qquad
\begin{array}{r} 297 \\ +493 \\ \hline \end{array}
\qquad
\begin{array}{r} 386 \\ +857 \\ \hline \end{array}
$$

2.
$$
\begin{array}{r} 3,333 \\ +\ \ \ 777 \\ \hline \end{array}
\qquad
\begin{array}{r} 9,054 \\ +\ \ \ 857 \\ \hline \end{array}
\qquad
\begin{array}{r} 3,289 \\ +1,931 \\ \hline \end{array}
\qquad
\begin{array}{r} 8,721 \\ +1,189 \\ \hline \end{array}
$$

Write and solve an equation for each problem.

3. Miguel is a mousetrap maker. Once he made **563** mousetraps out of
bubblegum. He made another **447** mousetraps out of doorknobs.
Quite the clever fellow! How many did he make in all?

_____

4. Luis spends all day thinking. One day he thought of **1,599** funny jokes
to tell his friends. His friend Pedro thought of **2,735** very funny jokes to tell.
Was there ever a lot of laughing that day! How many jokes did their
friends hear?

_____

Add with more than one regrouping

Add Three or More Numbers

When adding more than two numbers, look for sums of ten in each column to help you.

Add the **ones**. Regroup as needed.	Add the **tens**. Regroup as needed.	Add the **hundreds**. Regroup as needed.	Add the **thousands**. Regroup as needed.

¹
```
    51        Look for
 3,436       sums of 10.
+  359       1 + 9 = 10
─────────
     6
```

^{1 1}
```
    51        Look for
 3,436       sums of 10.
+  359       5 + 5 = 10
─────────
    46
```

^{1 1}
```
    51
 3,436
+  359
─────────
   846
```

^{1 1}
```
    51
 3,436
+  359
─────────
 3,846
```

Add. Regroup as needed.

1.
```
   12          70           4          325
    6          19          59          163
+  94        + 31        + 46        + 785
```

2.
```
  105         392       3,162        1,322
  347          47       6,392          411
+  55        + 741     + 4,818       +   78
```

Rewrite as a vertical problem. Then **add**.

3. 46 + 127 + 34   502 + 88 + 9   456 + 2,453 + 78   4,567 + 89 + 123

Solve the problem.

4. Melinda loved to read. First, she read a book about Mexico with **250** pages. Then, she read a joke book with **97** pages. Last, she read a poetry book with **453** pages. How many pages did she read? _____

Subtract Greater Numbers

Subtract the ones.

$$\begin{array}{r} 2\;14 \\ 2\cancel{3}\cancel{4} \\ -\,1\,4\,8 \\ \hline 6 \end{array}$$

4 – 8 = ? Regroup
3 tens and 4 ones
to **2** tens and **14**
ones.

Subtract the tens.

$$\begin{array}{r} 1\;12 \\ 2\cancel{3}\,14 \\ 2\cancel{3}\cancel{4} \\ -\,1\,4\,8 \\ \hline 8\,6 \end{array}$$

2 – 4 = ? Regroup
2 hundreds and 2
tens to **1** hundred
and **12** tens.

Subtract the hundreds.

$$\begin{array}{r} 1\;12 \\ \cancel{2}\cancel{3}\,14 \\ 2\cancel{3}\cancel{4} \\ -\,1\,4\,8 \\ \hline 8\,6 \end{array}$$

1 – 1 = 0, but do not
write a leading zero
in a **whole number**.

Subtract. Regroup as needed.

1.
$$\begin{array}{r} 736 \\ -\,349 \\ \hline \end{array} \qquad \begin{array}{r} 8{,}127 \\ -\,675 \\ \hline \end{array} \qquad \begin{array}{r} 7{,}194 \\ -\,1{,}856 \\ \hline \end{array} \qquad \begin{array}{r} 340 \\ -\,93 \\ \hline \end{array}$$

2.
$$\begin{array}{r} 6{,}354 \\ -\,5{,}888 \\ \hline \end{array} \qquad \begin{array}{r} 3{,}447 \\ -\,1{,}299 \\ \hline \end{array} \qquad \begin{array}{r} 4{,}253 \\ -\,2{,}444 \\ \hline \end{array} \qquad \begin{array}{r} 9{,}876 \\ -\,3{,}877 \\ \hline \end{array}$$

3.
$$\begin{array}{r} 1{,}623 \\ -\,766 \\ \hline \end{array} \qquad \begin{array}{r} 7{,}561 \\ -\,2{,}654 \\ \hline \end{array} \qquad \begin{array}{r} 6{,}276 \\ -\,559 \\ \hline \end{array} \qquad \begin{array}{r} 1{,}784 \\ -\,795 \\ \hline \end{array}$$

Subtract with Zeros

Subtract the ones.

$$\begin{array}{r} {\scriptstyle\downarrow} \\ 5{,}500 \\ +\ 2{,}376 \\ \hline ? \end{array}$$

Since there are no tens to regroup, regroup the hundreds.

Regroup the hundreds to show more tens.

$$\begin{array}{r} {\scriptstyle 4\ 10} \\ 5{,}\cancel{5}\cancel{0}0 \\ -\ 2{,}376 \\ \hline ? \end{array}$$

You still need more ones to subtract. Regroup the tens.

Regroup the tens to show more ones.

$$\begin{array}{r} {\scriptstyle\ \ 9\ 10} \\ {\scriptstyle 4\ 1\cancel{0}} \\ 5{,}\cancel{5}\cancel{0}\cancel{0} \\ -\ 2{,}376 \\ \hline 4 \end{array}$$

Now you can subtract the ones.
$10 - 6 = 4$

Finish the subtracting.

$$\begin{array}{r} {\scriptstyle\ \ 9\ 10} \\ {\scriptstyle 4\ 1\cancel{0}} \\ 5{,}\cancel{5}\cancel{0}\cancel{0} \\ -\ 2{,}376 \\ \hline 3{,}124 \end{array}$$

Check:

$$\begin{array}{r} {\scriptstyle 1\ \ 1} \\ 3{,}124 \\ +\ 2{,}376 \\ \hline 5{,}500 \end{array}$$

Regroup to show more ones.

1. 6 0 2   4 0 0   7,0 0 5   4,0 0 0

Subtract. Regroup carefully. Check you answers by adding.

2.
$$\begin{array}{r} 204 \\ -\ 117 \\ \hline \end{array} \qquad \begin{array}{r} 408 \\ -\ 29 \\ \hline \end{array} \qquad \begin{array}{r} 800 \\ -\ 529 \\ \hline \end{array} \qquad \begin{array}{r} 503 \\ -\ 56 \\ \hline \end{array}$$

3.
$$\begin{array}{r} 6{,}700 \\ -\ 5{,}379 \\ \hline \end{array} \qquad \begin{array}{r} 7{,}020 \\ -\ 443 \\ \hline \end{array} \qquad \begin{array}{r} 5{,}002 \\ -\ 661 \\ \hline \end{array} \qquad \begin{array}{r} 6{,}000 \\ -\ 1{,}278 \\ \hline \end{array}$$

4. In **1521**, Hernando Cortes conquered Mexico for the country of Spain. Then in the year **1810**, Miguel Hidalgo y Costilla fought for Mexico's freedom from Spain. How many years did Spain rule Mexico before they began to fight for their freedom?

_____

Numbers, Adding, and Subtracting

Across

1. 50,000 + 300 + 70 + 5

5. 794 – 258

7. 403 – 319

8. 5,821 – ____ = 5,725

9. 1,375 to the nearest hundred

11. 9,000 – 1,281

13. 372 + ____ = 450

14. 1,000 – 729

15. sixty-one thousand three hundred eight

Down

1. five thousand seventeen

2. 375 to the nearest ten

3. 7,429 to the nearest hundred

4. 63 = ____ tens and 13 ones

5. 44,428 + 12,345

6. 483 + 37 + 109

8. 4,755 + 4,966

10. 400 + 6 + 80

12. 789 – 679

Review whole numbers, adding, and subtracting   11

Multiply with Regrouping

Multiply the **ones**. Regroup as needed.	Multiply the **tens**. Regroup as needed.	Multiply the **hundreds**.	Estimate to check.
1 415 x 3 —— 5	1 415 x 3 —— 45	1 415 x 3 —— 1,245	400 x 3 —— 1,200
3 x 5 ones =15 ones Regroup 15 ones as 1 ten and 5 ones.	3 x 1 ten = 3 tens 3 tens + 1 ten = 4 tens	3 x 4 hundreds = 12 hundreds	1,200 is close to the exact product 1,245.

Multiply. Regroup as needed.

1.
$$\begin{array}{r} 58 \\ \times\ 4 \\ \hline \end{array} \qquad \begin{array}{r} 17 \\ \times\ 6 \\ \hline \end{array} \qquad \begin{array}{r} 73 \\ \times\ 8 \\ \hline \end{array} \qquad \begin{array}{r} 46 \\ \times\ 9 \\ \hline \end{array} \qquad \begin{array}{r} 92 \\ \times\ 7 \\ \hline \end{array}$$

2.
$$\begin{array}{r} 272 \\ \times\ 3 \\ \hline \end{array} \qquad \begin{array}{r} 971 \\ \times\ 7 \\ \hline \end{array} \qquad \begin{array}{r} 381 \\ \times\ 2 \\ \hline \end{array} \qquad \begin{array}{r} 812 \\ \times\ 4 \\ \hline \end{array} \qquad \begin{array}{r} 619 \\ \times\ 8 \\ \hline \end{array}$$

3.
$$\begin{array}{r} 1,522 \\ \times\ 3 \\ \hline \end{array} \qquad \begin{array}{r} 4,314 \\ \times\ 2 \\ \hline \end{array} \qquad \begin{array}{r} 9,171 \\ \times\ 6 \\ \hline \end{array} \qquad \begin{array}{r} 3,115 \\ \times\ 8 \\ \hline \end{array} \qquad \begin{array}{r} 4,123 \\ \times\ 9 \\ \hline \end{array}$$

4. There are **24** hours in a day. There are **7** days in one week. How many hours are there in one week.

5. It is **472** miles between Houston, Texas and Mobile, Alabama. How many miles is a round trip?

_____   _____

Multiply with Zeros

Multiply the **ones**. Regroup as needed.	Multiply the **tens**. Regroup as needed.	Multiply the **hundreds**.
$\overset{2}{5}04$ $\times\quad 6$ ——— $\qquad 4$	$\overset{2}{5}04$ $\times\quad 6$ ——— $\quad 24$	$\overset{2}{5}04$ $\times\quad 6$ ——— $3{,}024$
6 x 4 ones = 24 ones 24 ones = 2 tens and 4 ones.	6 x 0 tens = 0 tens 0 tens + 2 tens = 2 tens	6 x 5 hundreds = 30 hundreds

Multiply. Regroup as needed.

1.
$$560 \times 5$$
$$601 \times 8$$
$$302 \times 5$$
$$809 \times 3$$

2.
$$2{,}002 \times 7$$
$$7{,}050 \times 4$$
$$8{,}007 \times 2$$
$$5{,}060 \times 9$$

Solve each problem.

3. Many Mexican craft workers make beautiful pottery and glassware which they sell to tourists. If some tourists bought **8** pieces of pottery, and each piece sold for **$205**, how much money would the craft worker make? _____

4. The distance from Mexico City to Córdoba is about **170** miles. If a person made this trip **5** times, how many miles would he travel? _____

Multiply with zeros in the minuend, with regrouping

Multiply by Two-Digit Numbers

Multiply **by the ones** of the multiplier.	Multiply **by the tens** of the multiplier.	Add the **partial products.**	Estimate to check.
$\overset{1}{5}6$ $\times\ 23$ $\overline{168}$	$\overset{1}{5}6$ $\times\ \ 23$ $\overline{168}$ 1120	56 $\times\ \ 23$ $\overline{168}$ $+1120$ $\overline{1,288}$	60 $\times\ \ 20$ $\overline{1,200}$
23 is the multiplier. 3 x 56 = 168	20 x 56 = 1120		1,200 is close to the exact product, 1,288.

Find the **product.** Estimate to check your answers.

1.
```
   26        95        71        84
 x 13      x 48      x 32      x 59
```

2.
```
  332       816       194       776
 x  18     x  36     x  27     x  40
```

Multiply two-and three-digit numbers by two-digit numbers

Add, Subtract, and Multiply

Across

1. 8 x 67

4. 153 x 84

9. 150 x 5

10. 8,696 – 4,567

11. 299 + 202

12. 317 x 3

13. 3 x 202

14. ___ x 90 = 7,200

15. 4,876 + 9,321

Down

1. 238 + 337

2. 50 x 7

3. ___ x 20 = 12,020

5. 9,000 – 6,544

6. 747 + 47 + 17

7. 527 – 475

8. 59 x 50

14. 79 + 9

Two-Digit Quotients

Estimate.

$$20$$
$$4\overline{)95}$$

Think:
$4\overline{)8} = 2$
So, $4\overline{)80} = 20$

Making an estimate can help you place the first digit in the quotient.

Divide the tens.

$$2$$
$$4\overline{)95}$$
$$-8$$
$$\overline{1}$$

Divide: $4\overline{)9}$
Multiply: $4 \times 2 = 8$
Subtract: $9 - 8 = 1$
Compare: $1 < 4$

Bring down the ones. Repeat the steps to finish the dividing.

$$23$$
$$4\overline{)95}$$
$$-8\downarrow$$
$$\overline{15}$$
$$-12$$
$$\overline{3}$$

Divide: $4\overline{)15}$
Multiply: $4 \times 3 = 12$
Subtract: $15 - 12 = 3$
Compare: $3 < 4$
The remainder is 3.

The answer is **23 R3**.

Check:

$$23$$
$$\times 4$$
$$\overline{92}$$
$$+ 3$$
$$\overline{95}$$

Remember these steps:

1. Divide
2. Multiply
3. Subtract
4. Compare
5. Bring down

Repeat the steps until there are no more digits to bring down.

Divide. Check your answer.   Hint: There may or may not be remainders.

Check

1. $4\overline{)91}$ $6\overline{)89}$ $3\overline{)75}$

x _____   x _____   x _____

+ _____   + _____   + _____

Check

2. $7\overline{)84}$ $2\overline{)63}$ $5\overline{)96}$

x _____   x _____   x _____

+ _____   + _____   + _____

3. $6\overline{)75}$ $3\overline{)57}$ $8\overline{)87}$ $4\overline{)92}$ $5\overline{)99}$

Divide Three-Digit Numbers

When dividing a three-digit number by a one digit number, the quotient may have two or three digits. Study these two examples.

Estimate.

$$200$$
$$3\overline{)719}$$

Think:
$3\overline{)7}$ is close to $3\overline{)6}$.
$3\overline{)6} = 2$
So, $3\overline{)600} = 200$

Divide.

$$239\ R2$$
$$3\overline{)719}$$
$$-6$$
$$\overline{11}$$
$$-9$$
$$\overline{29}$$
$$-27$$
$$\overline{2}$$

1. **Divide**
2. **Multiply**
3. **Subtract**
4. **Compare**
5. **Bring down**

Repeat the steps as needed.

Estimate.

$$70$$
$$3\overline{)235}$$

Think:
$3\overline{)23}$ is close to $3\overline{)21}$.
$3\overline{)21} = 7$
So, $3\overline{)210} = 70$.

Divide.

$$78\ R1$$
$$3\overline{)235}$$
$$-21$$
$$\overline{25}$$
$$-24$$
$$\overline{1}$$

Estimate each quotient to the nearest ten or hundred.

1. $3\overline{)753}$ $5\overline{)173}$ $7\overline{)876}$ $8\overline{)333}$ $4\overline{)910}$

Divide. You might check your answers on another sheet of paper.

2. $3\overline{)753}$ $5\overline{)173}$ $7\overline{)876}$ $8\overline{)333}$ $4\overline{)910}$

3. $4\overline{)515}$ $3\overline{)264}$ $7\overline{)199}$ $5\overline{)590}$ $8\overline{)678}$

Zeros in the Quotient

Sometimes there are zeros in the quotient. Study these two examples.

Estimate.

$$\begin{array}{r} 200 \\ 3\overline{)622} \end{array}$$

Think:
$3\overline{)6} = 2$
So, $3\overline{)600} = 200$.

Divide.

$$\begin{array}{r} 207 \text{ R1} \\ 3\overline{)622} \\ -6 \\ \hline 02 \\ -0 \leftarrow 3 \times 0 = 0 \\ \hline 22 \\ -21 \\ \hline 1 \end{array}$$

Estimate.

$$\begin{array}{r} 40 \\ 6\overline{)244} \end{array}$$

Think:
$6\overline{)24} = 4$
So, $6\overline{)240} = 40$.

Divide.

$$\begin{array}{r} 40 \text{ R4} \\ 6\overline{)244} \\ -24 \\ \hline 04 \\ -0 \leftarrow 6 \times 0 = 0 \\ \hline 4 \end{array}$$

Estimate each quotient to the nearest ten or hundred.

1. $3\overline{)616}$ $\qquad$ $6\overline{)122}$ $\qquad$ $5\overline{)545}$ $\qquad$ $7\overline{)211}$ $\qquad$ $3\overline{)962}$

Divide. You might check your answers on another sheet of paper.

2. $3\overline{)616}$ $\qquad$ $6\overline{)122}$ $\qquad$ $5\overline{)545}$ $\qquad$ $7\overline{)211}$ $\qquad$ $3\overline{)962}$

3. $4\overline{)83}$ $\qquad$ $3\overline{)392}$ $\qquad$ $5\overline{)354}$ $\qquad$ $6\overline{)1,244}$ $\qquad$ $7\overline{)1,055}$

Divide with zeros in the quotients $\qquad\qquad$

Add, Subtract, Multiply, and Divide

Across

1. 43 x 9

4. 472 – 379

6. 609 + 225

7. 9)‾153‾

8. 13,003 – 3,425

10. ____ x 8 = 448

11. 466 + 905 + 95

14. 343 ÷ 7

16. 410 + 1,009 + 51 + 998

17. 8)‾384‾

18. 978 ÷ 6

Down

1. 763 x 5

2. 6)‾498‾

3. 58 + 7 + 684

4. 1,306 – 389

5. 97 x 39

9. 973 – 467

12. 576 ÷ 9

13. 208 x 3

15. 888 + 75

Understanding Fractions

Fractions can show parts of a whole, a set, or a line.
Study the examples below.

Part of a Whole:

$\dfrac{3}{4}$ ← colored parts
← total parts

In a whole, all the parts must be the same size.

Part of a Set:

$\dfrac{3}{4}$ ← colored objects
← total objects

In a set, the objects do not have to be the same size or shape.

Part of a Line:

$$\begin{array}{c} 0 \qquad\qquad 1 \end{array}$$

$\dfrac{0}{4} \quad \dfrac{1}{4} \quad \dfrac{2}{4} \quad \dfrac{3}{4} \quad \dfrac{4}{4}$

$\dfrac{3}{4}$ ← marks from 0
← total marks between 0 and 1

Think of a ruler when you work with a number line.

Write a fraction for the colored part of the whole or set.

1.

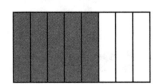 _____

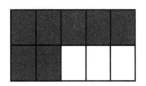 _____

2.

 _____

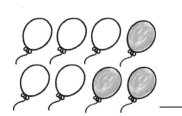 _____

 _____

Write a fraction to indicate where the red dot is on each number line.

3.

_____   _____   _____

Complete the picture to show each fraction.

4.

$\dfrac{3}{4}$

$\dfrac{2}{3}$

Equivalent Fractions

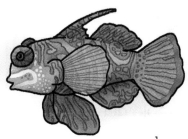

Equivalent fractions are fractions that name the same amount.
Here are some different ways to show fractions equivalent to $\frac{3}{4}$.

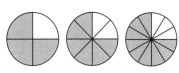

$$\frac{3}{4} = \frac{6}{8} = \frac{9}{12}$$

$\frac{3}{4}$

$\frac{6}{8}$

$\frac{9}{12}$

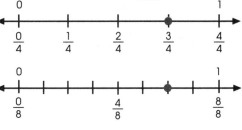

You can also multiply or divide the numerator and
denominator by the same number to find equivalent fractions.

$$\frac{3 \times 2}{4 \times 2} = \frac{6}{8} \qquad \frac{3 \times 3}{4 \times 3} = \frac{9}{12} \qquad \frac{6 \div 2}{8 \div 2} = \frac{3}{4}$$

Write the missing numerator.

1.

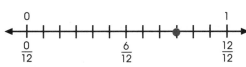

$$\frac{2}{3} = \frac{}{6} \qquad\qquad \frac{3}{4} = \frac{}{8} \qquad\qquad \frac{2}{5} = \frac{}{10}$$

2.

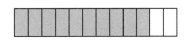

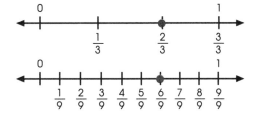

$$\frac{5}{6} = \frac{}{12} \qquad\qquad \frac{2}{3} = \frac{}{9} \qquad\qquad \frac{1}{6} = \frac{}{12}$$

Multiply or divide to find the equivalent fraction.

3.

$$\frac{2}{3} = \frac{}{15} \qquad \frac{3}{8} = \frac{}{16} \qquad \frac{1}{2} = \frac{}{12} \qquad \frac{8}{12} = \frac{}{3}$$

Mixed Numbers

A **mixed number** consists of a whole number and a fraction.

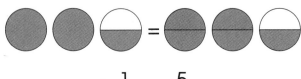

$$2\frac{1}{2} = \frac{5}{2}$$

An **improper fraction** consists of a numerator that is greater than or equal to the denominator.

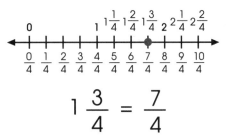

$$1\frac{3}{4} = \frac{7}{4}$$

Write an improper fraction and a mixed number in simplest form for each picture.

1. _____ = _____

 _____ = _____

2.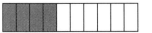

 _____ = _____

 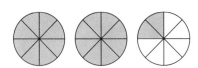

 _____ = _____

Write a whole number or a mixed number in simplest form for each improper fraction.

3. $\dfrac{5}{4}$ = _____ $\dfrac{9}{6}$ = _____ $\dfrac{6}{3}$ = _____ $\dfrac{10}{8}$ = _____

4. $\dfrac{7}{7}$ = _____ $\dfrac{9}{4}$ = _____ $\dfrac{16}{5}$ = _____ $\dfrac{10}{4}$ = _____

Compare Fractions

To compare fractions, you can look at pictures or objects or use equivalent fractions.

Which is greater, $\dfrac{3}{4}$ or $\dfrac{5}{8}$?

Example 1:

$\dfrac{3}{4}$

$\dfrac{5}{8}$

You can see that $\dfrac{3}{4} > \dfrac{5}{8}$.

Example 2:

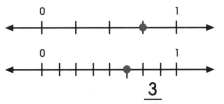

You can see that $\dfrac{3}{4}$ is further away from zero. So, $\dfrac{3}{4} > \dfrac{5}{8}$.

Example 3: Find equivalent fractions with a common denominator. Compare the numerators.

$$\dfrac{3}{4} = \dfrac{6}{8} \qquad \dfrac{5}{8} = \dfrac{5}{8}$$

$$\dfrac{6}{8} > \dfrac{5}{8}$$

So, $\dfrac{3}{4} > \dfrac{5}{8}$

Compare the fractions. Write <, >, or = in the ⬤ .

1.

$\dfrac{6}{8}$ ⬤ $\dfrac{1}{2}$

$\dfrac{2}{3}$ ⬤ $\dfrac{6}{9}$

$\dfrac{1}{3}$ ⬤ $\dfrac{1}{2}$

Complete the fraction pictures to show the fractions in each problem.
Compare the fractions and then write <, >, or = in the ⬤ .

2.

$\dfrac{3}{4}$ ⬤ $\dfrac{3}{8}$

$\dfrac{2}{3}$ ⬤ $\dfrac{8}{12}$

$\dfrac{1}{3}$ ⬤ $\dfrac{5}{6}$

Compare. Write <, >, or = in the ⬤ .

3. $\dfrac{4}{6}$ ⬤ $\dfrac{1}{3}$ $\dfrac{3}{6}$ ⬤ $\dfrac{5}{10}$ $\dfrac{3}{5}$ ⬤ $\dfrac{1}{2}$ $\dfrac{1}{2}$ ⬤ $\dfrac{3}{8}$

4. $\dfrac{3}{6}$ ⬤ $\dfrac{3}{4}$ $\dfrac{1}{2}$ ⬤ $\dfrac{1}{4}$ $\dfrac{1}{3}$ ⬤ $\dfrac{3}{4}$ $\dfrac{3}{4}$ ⬤ $\dfrac{4}{5}$

    Compare like and unlike fractions

Add Fractions with Unlike Denominators

To add fractions with unlike denominators:

- *First find equivalent fractions.*
- Add the numerators. The denominator remains the same.
- Write the sum in simplest form.

What is $\frac{1}{2} + \frac{1}{3}$?

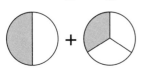

$\frac{1}{2} + \frac{1}{3} = ?$

$\frac{1}{2} = \frac{3}{6}$

$\frac{1}{3} = \frac{2}{6}$

$\frac{3}{6} + \frac{2}{6} = \frac{5}{6}$

The sum is $\frac{5}{6}$.

Find equivalent fractions.

$\frac{1}{2} + \frac{1}{3}$

$\downarrow \qquad \downarrow$

$\frac{3}{6} + \frac{2}{6} = \frac{5}{6}$

The sum is $\frac{5}{6}$.

Add the fractions. Write the sum in simplest form. Show your work.

1. $\frac{1}{6} + \frac{1}{2}$

$\downarrow \qquad \downarrow$

_____ + _____ = _____

$\frac{1}{4} + \frac{3}{8}$

$\downarrow \qquad \downarrow$

_____ + _____ = _____

$\frac{1}{8} + \frac{1}{2}$

$\downarrow \qquad \downarrow$

_____ + _____ = _____

2. $\frac{1}{3} + \frac{1}{6} =$ _____

$\frac{3}{4} + \frac{1}{8} =$ _____

$\frac{5}{12} + \frac{1}{3} =$ _____

3. $\frac{1}{4} + \frac{3}{6} =$ _____

$\frac{2}{5} + \frac{1}{2} =$ _____

$\frac{2}{3} + \frac{1}{6} =$ _____

4. A recipe calls for $\frac{1}{4}$ cup of walnuts and $\frac{1}{2}$ cup of pecans. How many cups of nuts are needed for this recipe? _____

Subtract Fractions with Unlike Denominators

To subtract fractions with unlike denominators:

- *First find equivalent fractions.*
- Subtract the numerators. The denominator remains the same.
- Write the difference in simplest form.

What is $\dfrac{3}{4} - \dfrac{1}{8}$?

$\dfrac{3}{4} - \dfrac{1}{8} = ?$

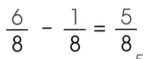

$\dfrac{6}{8} - \dfrac{1}{8} = \dfrac{5}{8}$

The difference is $\dfrac{5}{8}$.

Find equivalent fractions.

$$\dfrac{3}{4} \quad - \quad \dfrac{1}{8}$$
$$\downarrow \qquad \downarrow$$
$$\dfrac{6}{8} - \dfrac{1}{8} = \dfrac{5}{8}$$

The difference is $\dfrac{5}{8}$.

Subtract the fractions. Write the difference in simplest form. Show your work.

1. $\dfrac{5}{8} - \dfrac{1}{2}$ 　　　　　 $\dfrac{3}{4} - \dfrac{1}{8}$ 　　　　　 $\dfrac{5}{6} - \dfrac{3}{4}$

$$\downarrow \quad \downarrow \qquad\qquad \downarrow \quad \downarrow \qquad\qquad \downarrow \quad \downarrow$$

_____ - _____ = _____　　　 _____ - _____ = _____　　　 _____ - _____ = _____

2. $\dfrac{5}{6} - \dfrac{1}{3} =$ _____ 　　　 $\dfrac{7}{10} - \dfrac{1}{5} =$ _____ 　　　 $\dfrac{5}{12} - \dfrac{1}{3} =$ _____

3. $\dfrac{1}{4} - \dfrac{1}{12} =$ _____ 　　　 $\dfrac{4}{5} - \dfrac{1}{2} =$ _____ 　　　 $\dfrac{2}{3} - \dfrac{1}{6} =$ _____

4. Andy has two miniature cars. The blue car is $\dfrac{3}{4}$ inches long and the red car is $\dfrac{5}{8}$ inches long.

Which car is longer? _____

How much longer? _____

Decimal Place Value

fraction	meaning	tens	ones		tenths	hundreds	decimal	word name
$\frac{3}{10}$			0	.	3		0.3	three tenths
$\frac{3}{100}$			0	.	0	3	0.03	three hundredths
$2\frac{7}{10}$			2	.	7		2.7	two *and* seven tenths
$1\frac{62}{100}$			1	.	6	2	1.62	one *and* sixty-two hundredths

Say "and" for the decimal point.

Write the **fraction or mixed number** and **decimal** for the colored part of each picture.

1.  _____ , _____

2.  _____ , _____

3. _____ , _____

4.  _____ , _____

Write the **decimal** for each number name.

5. three and eight tenths _____   thirty–eight hundredths _____

6. five and seven hundredths _____   fifty-seven hundredths _____

Tell the **place value** of the **5** in each number.

7. 3.5 _____   5.3 _____

8. 3.25 _____   53.7 _____

Compare and Order Decimals

Compare **2.38** and **2.8**

Line up the
decimal points.

↓
2.38
2.8

$2.8 = 2.80$

Begin at the left. Find the first
place where the digits are
different. Then compare.

2.38
2.80
↑

3 tenths < 8 tenths   **2.38 < 2.8**

> means **greater than**
< means **less than**
= means **equal to**

The sign points to the
number that is less.

Compare the decimals. Write <, >, or = in the ○ .

1. 0.7 ○ 0.07   0.39 ○ 3.9   3.15 ○ 3.5

2. 4.5 ○ 4.50   4.5 ○ 4.05   2.99 ○ 3

3. 3.01 ○ 301.   8.53 ○ 85.3   6 ○ 6.00

Write the decimals in **order** from **least to greatest**.

4. 0.38 8.3 0.83 3.8   _____

5. 1.05 0.15 1.5 15   _____

6. 0.7 0.07 7 70.0   _____

7. 0.02 0.22 0.2 2.0   _____

8. 346.1 34.61 3,461 346.01   _____

Add Decimals

Add **3.8**, **1.53**, and **6**

Line up the decimal points. Write equivalent decimals as needed.

Add like whole numbers. Regroup as needed.

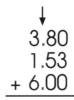

> Remember the decimal point is at the end of a whole number.
> 6 = 6.0 or 6.00

$$\begin{array}{r} \downarrow \\ 3.80 \\ 1.53 \\ + 6.00 \\ \hline \end{array}$$

$$\begin{array}{r} 1 \\ 3.80 \\ 1.53 \\ + 6.00 \\ \hline 11.33 \end{array}$$

Add the decimals.

1.
$$\begin{array}{r} 5.9 \\ + 3.7 \\ \hline \end{array}$$
$$\begin{array}{r} 6.38 \\ + 0.5 \\ \hline \end{array}$$
$$\begin{array}{r} 0.7 \\ + 0.65 \\ \hline \end{array}$$
$$\begin{array}{r} 4.09 \\ + 3.91 \\ \hline \end{array}$$
$$\begin{array}{r} \$23.65 \\ + \ \$9.71 \\ \hline \end{array}$$

2.
$$\begin{array}{r} 7.38 \\ 4.6 \\ + 0.38 \\ \hline \end{array}$$
$$\begin{array}{r} 6.7 \\ 8 \\ + 0.49 \\ \hline \end{array}$$
$$\begin{array}{r} 23.5 \\ 2.35 \\ + \ 0.02 \\ \hline \end{array}$$
$$\begin{array}{r} 4.6 \\ 4.06 \\ + 46 \\ \hline \end{array}$$
$$\begin{array}{r} 3.0 \\ 0.3 \\ + 3.03 \\ \hline \end{array}$$

Rewrite as a vertical problem. Then **add.**

3. 3.8 + 0.62   40.8 + 4.08   9.3 + 7 $4.37 + $1.99 $7.09 + $8

4. 1.5 + 8 + 2.05   1.5 + 0.15 + 5.1   6.7 + 67 + 0.67   7.3 + 73 + 0.73

Subtract Decimals

Subtract: 5.3 – 2.18	Line up the decimal points. Write equivalent decimals as needed.	Subtract whole numbers. Regroup as needed.	Check your answer.

$$\begin{array}{r} 5.30 \\ -\ 2.18 \\ \hline \end{array}$$

$$\begin{array}{r} {\scriptstyle 2\,10} \\ 5.\cancel{3}\cancel{0} \\ -\ 2.18 \\ \hline 3.12 \end{array}$$

$$\begin{array}{r} {\scriptstyle 1} \\ 3.12 \\ +\ 2.18 \\ \hline 5.30 \end{array}$$

Subtract the decimals.

1.
$$\begin{array}{r} 8.3 \\ -\ 1.5 \\ \hline \end{array} \qquad \begin{array}{r} 4.58 \\ -\ 3.9 \\ \hline \end{array} \qquad \begin{array}{r} 6.5 \\ -\ 0.79 \\ \hline \end{array} \qquad \begin{array}{r} \$5.25 \\ -\ \$1.79 \\ \hline \end{array} \qquad \begin{array}{r} \$8.50 \\ -\ \$3.99 \\ \hline \end{array}$$

Rewrite as a vertical problem. Then **subtract**.

2. 6.5 – 3.8   7.05 – 1.9   9 – 3.7   9.2 – 0.92 $20 – $4.83

Solve each problem.

3. Miss James has **59.3** acres of land. She bought **25** more acres. How much land does she have now?

4. Kevin bought a belt for **$5.39**. He paid for it with a **$10**-bill. How much change should he get?

What I Learned about Whole Numbers

Write each number in **standard form**.

1. 50,000 + 7,000 + 200 + 60 + 8 _____

2. 700,000 + 4,000 + 80 _____

3. eighty million, four hundred eleven thousand, nine _____

4. seventy-three thousand, four hundred forty _____

Write each number in **expanded form**.

5. 62,017 _____

6. 430,205 _____

Tell the **place value** of the **8** in each number.

7. 3,585,146 _____

8. 508,507,506 _____

Compare. Write <, >, or = in the ⬤.

9. 5,218 ⬤ 5,281   79,260 ⬤ 709,026   5 x 12 ⬤ 4 x 15

Order the numbers from **least to greatest**.

10. 456,894   465,894   456,984   465,498 _____

_____

Round each number to the place shown.

11. 513 (hundreds) _____   375 (tens) _____

12. 45,099 (thousands) _____   372,055 (hundreds) _____

Answer Key

Page 1

1. 57,269
2. 305,806
3. 740,053
4. 30,000 + 4,000 + 500 + 60 + 2
5. 600,000 + 20,000 + 1,000 + 700
6. 400,000 + 3,000 + 80 + 7
7. thirty-five thousand, six hundred twenty-one
8. two hundred forty-six thousand, eight hundred nine

Page 2

1. 9,103,205
2. 433,647,112
3. 17,221,050
4. 7 ten-millions
5. 7 millions
6. 7 thousands
7. 7 ten-thousands
8. 7 tens
9. 7 hundred-millions

Page 3

1. > 2. > 3. >
   <   <   =
   <   <   <
4. 149; 287; 324; 822
5. 2,118; 2,973; 3,006; 3,652
6. 2,821; 2,840; 4,431; 4,931
7.

	100	200	300	400	500
	135		310		460

Juanita Lucia Maria

Page 4

1. 40; 90; 60
2. 390; 250; 810
3. 1,280; 4,070; 8,760
4. 400; 500; 400
5. 1,900; 2,500; 7,500
6. 100; 100; 0
7. $2; $8; $28

Page 5

1. 3,000; 7,000; 8,000
2. 15,000; 41,000; 30,000
3. 1,000; 0; 0
4. 19,000; 18,000; 12,000; 7,000
5. 761,610; 761,600;
   762,000; 760,000;
   800,000; 1,000,000

Page 6

1. 81; 81; 72; 73
2. 792; 902; 950; 963
3. 4,632; 8,358; 6,288; 9,628
4. 45 + 45 = 90 minutes
5. 365 + 283 = 648 apples

Page 7

1. 961; 1,261; 790; 1,243
2. 4,110; 9,911; 5,220; 9,910
3. 563 + 447 = 1,010 mousetraps
4. 1,599 + 2,735 = 4,334 jokes

Page 8

1. 112; 120; 109; 1,273
2. 507; 1,180; 14,372; 1,811
3. 207; 599; 2,987; 4,779
4. 800 pages

Page 9

1. 387; 7,452; 5,338; 247
2. 466; 2,148; 1,809; 5,999
3. 857; 4,907; 5,717; 989

Page 10

1. 602 400 7,005 4,000
2. 87; 379; 271; 447
3. 1,321; 6,577; 4,341 4,722
4. 289 years

Page 11

1. 5	0	2. 3	3. 7	4. 5		5. 5	3	6. 6
0		7. 8	4		8. 9	6		2
9. 1	10. 4	0	0		11. 7	7	12. 1	9
13. 7	8		0		14. 2	7	1	
	6			15. 6	1	3	0	8

Page 12

1. 232; 102; 584; 414; 644
2. 816; 6,797; 762; 3,248; 4,952
3. 4,566; 8,628; 55,026; 24,920; 37,107
4. 168 hours
5. 944 miles

Page 13

1. 2,800; 4,808; 1,510; 2,427
2. 14,014; 28,200; 16,014; 45,540
3. $1,640
4. 850 miles

Page 14

1. 338; 4,560; 2,272; 4,956
2. 5,976; 29,376; 5,238; 31,040

Page 15

1. 5	2. 3	3. 6		4. 1	5. 2	6. 8	7. 5	8. 2
9. 7	5	0			10. 4	1	2	9
11. 5	0	1		12. 9	5	1		5
		13. 6	0	6			14. 8	0
15. 1	4	1	9	7			8	

Answer Key

Page 16

1. 22 R3   14 R5   25
2. 12   31 R1   19 R1
3. 12 R3   19   10 R7   23   19 R4

Page 17

1. 300   30   100   40   200
2. 251   34 R3   125 R1   41 R5   227 R2
3. 128 R3   88   28 R3   118   84 R6

Page 18

1. 200   20   100   30   300
2. 205 R1   20 R2   109   30 R1   320 R2
3. 20 R3   130 R2   70 R4   207R2   150 R5

Page 19

1. 3	2. 8	3. 7		4. 9	5. 3
6. 8	3	4	7. 1		7
1		8. 9	9. 5	7	8
10. 5	6		0		3
	11. 1	4	6	12. 6	
13. 6				14. 4	15. 9
16. 2	4	6	8		6
17. 4	8		18. 1	6	3

Page 20

1. 5/8   5/6   7/10
2. 7/12   2/3   3/8
3. 2/5   5/9   11/12
4. 5/6 ⬡   3/4 🌸🌸   2/3 ⟵|——|——|——⟶ 0 1/3 2/3 3/3

Page 21

1. 2/3 = 4/6   3/4 = 6/8   2/5 = 4/10
2. 5/6 = 10/12   2/3 = 6/9   1/6 = 2/12
3. 2/3 = 10/15   3/8 = 6/16   1/2 = 6/12
   8/12 = 2/3

Page 22

1. 5/3 = 1 2/3   14/10 = 1 2/5
2. 8/6 = 1 1/3   18/8 = 2 1/4
3. 1 1/4   1 1/2   2   1 1/4
4. 1   2 1/4   3 1/5   2 1/2

Page 23

1. >   =   <

2.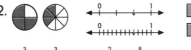
   $\frac{3}{4} > \frac{3}{8}$ $\frac{2}{3} = \frac{8}{12}$ $\frac{1}{3} < \frac{5}{6}$

3. >   =   >   >
4. <   >   <   <

Page 24

1. 1/6 + 3/6 = 4/6 = 2/3
   2/8 + 3/8 = 5/8
   1/8 + 4/8 = 5/8
2. 1/2   7/8   3/4
3. 3/4   9/10   5/6
4. 3/4 cup

Page 25

1. 5/8 - 4/8 = 1/8
   6/8 - 1/8 = 5/8
   10/12 - 9/12 = 1/12
2. 1/2   1/2   1/12
3. 1/6   3/10   1/2
4. blue car,   1/8 inch

Page 26

1. 9/10, 0.9
2. 9/100, 0.09
3. 1 3/10, 1.3
4. 1 31/100, 1.31
5. 3.8   0.38
6. 5.07   0.57
7. tenths, ones
8. hundredths, tens

Page 27

1. >   <   <
2. =   >   <
3. <   <   =
4. 0.38   0.83   3.8   8.3
5. 0.15   1.05   1.5   15
6. 0.07   0.7   7   70.0
7. 0.02   0.2   0.22   2.0
8. 34.61   346.01   346.1   3,461

Page 28

1. 9.6   6.88   1.35   8.00 or 8 $33.36
2. 12.36   15.19   25.87   54.66   6.33
3. 4.42   44.88   16.3 $6.36 $15.09
4. 11.55   6.75   74.37   81.03

Page 29

1. 6.8   0.68   5.71 $3.46 $4.51
2. 2.7   5.15   5.3   8.28 $15.17
3. 84.3 acres
4. $4.61

Page 30

1. 57, 268
2. 704, 080
3. 80, 411, 009
4. 73,440
5. 60,000 + 2,000 + 10 + 7
6. 400,000 + 30,000 + 200 + 5
7. ten-thousands
8. one millions
9. <   <   =
10. 456,894   456,984   465,498   465,894
11. 500   380
12. 45,000   372,100